Careers for Creative People

Careers in the Culinary Arts

Peggy J. Parks

ReferencePoint
Press®

San Diego, CA

© 2020 ReferencePoint Press, Inc.
Printed in the United States

For more information, contact:
ReferencePoint Press, Inc.
PO Box 27779
San Diego, CA 92198
www.ReferencePointPress.com

LIBRARY OF CONGRESS CATALOGING-IN-PUBLICATION DATA

Name: Parks, Peggy J., 1951– author.
Title: Careers in the Culinary Arts/by Peggy J. Parks.
Description: San Diego, CA: ReferencePoint Press, Inc., 2020. | Series:
Careers for Creative People | Includes bibliographical references and
index. | Audience: Grades 9 to 12.
Identifiers: LCCN 2019004408 (print) | LCCN 2019008365 (ebook) | ISBN
9781682826782 (eBook) | ISBN 9781682826775 (hardback)
Subjects: LCSH: Food service—Vocational guidance—Juvenile literature. |
Cooking—Vocational guidance—Juvenile literature.
Classification: LCC TX911.3.V62 (ebook) | LCC TX911.3.V62 P36 2020 (print) |
DDC 642/.4023—dc23
LC record available at https://lccn.loc.gov/2019004408

Contents

Careers for Creative Foodies

Creative people exhibit their artistry in a number of different ways. Some paint landscapes or portraits, and others design clothing, create video games, take photographs, compose music, or write books. Creative people who love food may display their passion through a different sort of artistry, as renowned chef, public speaker, and author Chris Hill explains in an article on the Medium website: "One of the most important things an artist does is see things that don't yet exist, and finds ways to bring them to life—that's what we do through our food, our menus and our restaurants." People with careers that are in some way connected to food are part of a field known as the culinary arts.

The Cookery Hierarchy

A variety of careers fall under the culinary arts umbrella, but chef is the one that typically comes to mind when people think about the field. Although it is common for the terms *chef* and *cook* to be used interchangeably, they are two different jobs. Cooks are the food preparers and are supervised by chefs, who may or may not participate in the actual cooking.

Chefs often have different titles depending on their chosen specialty, level of talent, and years of experience. An executive chef (or head chef) is at the very top of a kitchen hierarchy in a restaurant or other food establishment. He or she is ultimately responsible for everything from menu development and oversight of food preparation to training and supervising cooks and other kitchen staff. In larger, more exclusive restaurants, many of the executive chef's administrative tasks are delegated to the sous-chef, who is the second-in-command. The complete title is *sous-chef de cuisine*, which is French for "under-chef of the kitchen."

A highly specialized type of chef is a pastry chef. These artistic professionals create delectable baked goods and confections, including fancy layer cakes, pies, tarts, specialty desserts, and breads. Dolester Miles from Birmingham, Alabama, has been a pastry chef for more than thirty years. She oversees a staff of four and the baking production of four restaurants under the same ownership. Miles is widely known and beloved for her incomparable desserts, such as a three-layer coconut-pecan cake with Chantilly cream frosting, a lemon meringue tart, a sweet potato pie, and fresh peach and blueberry cobblers.

Miles's reputation as a superb pastry chef extends far beyond her hometown. In May 2018 she was presented with that year's coveted James Beard Foundation Outstanding Pastry Chef award. "I never dreamed they would call my name," Miles said in an October 2018 *Washington Post* story. "To win, it's a feeling that I can't even explain. . . . It was amazing. I still think about it and cry."

Exciting Variety

Although traditional careers such as chef are most often associated with the culinary arts, the field is actually quite varied—and many positions have little (or nothing) to do with cooking. On its website, the Culinary Institute of America writes, "In the past, working in food typically meant becoming a restaurant chef. But today, it's hard to even keep track of the diverse range of opportunities in the culinary industry."

One example of a nontraditional culinary arts career is the craft brewer, also known as a brewmaster. These professionals own and operate small independent breweries, where they produce their own unique brand of custom-crafted beer. The food writer is another less-traditional career in the culinary arts. Food writers write and edit articles for all kinds of print and digital publications, including gourmet food and general interest magazines,

Careers in the Culinary Arts

Occupation	Minimum Educational Requirement	2017 Median Salary
Chef and head cook	High school diploma or equivalent	$45,950
Food service manager	High school diploma or equivalent	$52,030
Cook	High school diploma or equivalent	$23,970
Waiter and waitress	No formal educational requirement	$20,820
Food and beverage server and related worker	No formal educational requirement	$20,410
Baker	No formal educational requirement	$25,690
Dietitian and nutritionist	Bachelor's degree	$59,410
Agricultural and food scientist	Bachelor's degree	$62,910
Food preparation worker	No formal educational requirement	$22,730

Source: Bureau of Labor Statistics, *Occupational Outlook Handbook*, 2019. www.bls.gov.

cookbooks, newspaper food sections, and food blogs, just to name a few. The same kinds of publications use color photos taken by food photographers, which is another culinary arts career. Or, those whose talents lean toward design may want to explore becoming food stylists, who make food look gorgeous and irresistible in the photos taken by food photographers. Creative foodies who love working with people may want to consider a career in food marketing or public relations.

The Future Beckons

Whatever their unique interests may be, creative foodies would benefit from exploring the culinary arts field. And industry experts say the future looks promising for many of these careers. There will, for instance, be a growing demand for traditional culinary professionals such as chefs and cooks in the coming years. The National Restaurant Association says its industry is adding jobs at a stronger rate than all other industries combined. The association projects that by 2027, the restaurant industry will add 1.6 million jobs throughout the United States, with the greatest amount of growth in the South and the West, especially in the states of Texas and Arizona.

Young people often have no idea what sort of career they want to pursue in the future, and that is perfectly normal. It can help—and be far less stressful—to start by focusing on personal interests and talents and building career plans from there. For those who are creative and passionate about food, the culinary arts field offers a wide variety of career options and is definitely worth exploring. As career expert Alison Doyle explains in an article on the Balance career website: "There's a whole world of opportunity for those passionate about the culinary arts."

Chef

Chefs are highly skilled professionals who are passionate about food and whose jobs are all about food. These are people who, through a combination of talent, experience, hard work, and acquired reputation, have reached one of the most prestigious positions in the culinary arts. One of them is Frank Proto, a chef from Long Island, New York, who knew from the time he was a child that he wanted to be a chef. "I know that's kind of weird—kids usually want to be firemen or policemen or lawyers," Proto commented in a June 2017 article on the Institute of Culinary Education (ICE) website. "I don't know where I got the idea but I always wanted to be a chef."

On his way up the career ladder, Proto worked at several different restaurants, which is typical of those who aspire to become chefs. Most continue working in restaurants throughout their careers, although chefs also work at other types of establishments where food is served. They are employed by country

At a Glance

Chef

Minimum Educational Requirements
High school diploma or equivalent

Personal Qualities
Passion for cooking; creativity; keen sense of taste and smell; business and leadership skills

Certification and Licensing
None required, but certification can show competence and lead to higher pay

Working Conditions
Inside the kitchens of restaurants or other establishments; environment is often extremely fast paced and can be dangerous

Salary Range
$25,000 to more than $78,500

Number of Jobs
About 146,500 in 2016

Future Job Outlook
Growth of 10 percent through 2026

8

clubs, cruise ships, resorts, and even hospitals. Some work as personal chefs for private individuals.

Chefs perform a wide variety of tasks and have much responsibility. Those who work for restaurants are charged with overseeing the kitchen, including everything that goes on in there and all the food that leaves it. Their specific duties vary based on the size of the establishment, but certain tasks are typical for most chefs. They plan menus, develop recipes, and ensure that food and ingredients are well stocked and fresh. They determine how food should be presented to patrons and ensure that it happens correctly and in a timely manner. Cleanliness and sanitation are vital for all food service establishments, and chefs monitor these practices carefully. They also hire, train, and supervise the work of everyone in the kitchen, from food preparation workers to cooks and sometimes other chefs.

While chefs are working, they use a variety of kitchen tools and equipment, including an assortment of knives. One is a chef's knife, which has a curved blade for fast cutting and chopping and a small tip for finer work. Chefs prize their knives and understand the importance of taking exceptional care of them by keeping them clean and sharpened using special stones. They also use many types and sizes of pots and pans as well as small kitchen gadgets such as spatulas, scrapers, and peelers. Appliances used by chefs include ranges, ovens, grills, griddles, fryers, and walk-in coolers and freezers.

Although no two days are necessarily identical, chefs often follow a routine and know (for the most part) what to expect from day to day. This is true of Chantelle Nicholson, who is the head chef and co-owner of a fine-dining restaurant in London called Tredwells. Nicholson usually works six days a week, and she arrives at the restaurant by 8:00 a.m. She greets her staff of twelve chefs, reviews the day's bookings, and then begins to sharpen knives and work on food preparation. Around midmorning, she makes breakfast for her team. This is usually bacon sandwiches or a Swiss cereal known as muesli, which is made with rolled oats, nuts, and fruit.

At about 11:00 a.m., each of Nicholson's chefs brings her a small portion of food that will be served that day to patrons; she tastes it and offers comments. At noon the restaurant starts to come alive with patrons arriving for lunch, and Nicholson oversees the service. She arranges food on plates for the main dishes (known as plating) and checks all food before it leaves the kitchen. After lunch, Tredwells slows down. "There's always a slight lull," explained Nicholson in a December 2017 interview on the website of *Good Housekeeping* magazine. "This is when I tend to send the team out for fresh air. I prefer not to take breaks myself as once I'm in the zone, it's easier to keep going." As evening approaches, things begin to pick up again. By 6:00 p.m. the restaurant is, as Nicholson describes, "a hive of activity."

Hours later, when all patrons have left the restaurant and it has been cleaned and the day's orders tallied, Nicholson finally goes home. It is not unusual for her to work fifteen-hour days, yet she would not trade her job for anything, as she says in the 2017 article: "Of course, it's exhausting, but it's highly rewarding too. . . . It's not just a career, it's a passion and a privilege to get paid for doing something I love."

How Do You Become a Chef?

Education

Chefs are typically not required to have a college degree, but many earn a bachelor's degree in the culinary arts. The American Culinary Federation accredits about two hundred of these programs throughout the United States. Although exact coursework can vary, classes often cover food science, food safety and sanitation, menu planning, baking and pastry making, food preparing, knife skills, international cooking, culinary entrepreneurship, and plating concepts.

Especially essential for an aspiring chef is experience—hands-on learning under the direction of an experienced chef. Those without a degree who aspire to be professional chefs often start at restaurants in lower-level positions. "You pretty much have to start at the bottom and work your way up to fully embrace and appreciate the process of being a chef and running a restaurant," says executive chef Anna Bran-Leis in a November 2017 article on *Food & Wine* magazine's website. "But it builds character and helps you appreciate the people doing the more painstaking jobs, like dishwashing. Every part of a kitchen has its own important role."

Certification and Licensing

Chefs are not typically required to be certified or licensed, but being certified by the American Culinary Federation can lead to higher-level positions and larger salaries. Depending on the certification, chefs must have a high school diploma or equivalent, have worked for a specified number of years on the job (usually three to five years), and received a passing score on written and practical exams.

Internships and Volunteer Work

Most culinary programs require one or more internships conducted in kitchens outside the school environment. Whether paid or not, these can provide aspiring chefs with invaluable on-the-job experience, as a March 2018 article on the culinary blog *Chefify* explains: "There are some incredibly skilled people at the top of the culinary profession and being around them can be very motivational. An internship is a fast track to seeing these great minds at work in their own environments, which may in turn inspire the rest of your career." Internships cover every aspect of cooking, from knife skills and kitchen equipment training to how to fix an entire meal from appetizers to dessert.

According to the Institute of Culinary Education (ICE), there are many volunteer opportunities for aspiring chefs. They can volunteer to help cook at charity events in their communities or at local rescue missions, soup kitchens, or homeless shelters. They can also help out with local food-related festivals. In an article on ICE's *Diced* blog, Lauren Jessen writes, "There are too many great volunteer opportunities to name, ranging from nonprofit work to glitzy events, weekly shifts to one-night commitments."

Volunteering in one's community can offer not only hands-on experience but also valuable opportunities to network with other culinary professionals.

Skills and Personality

Chefs are talented, artistic individuals who have achieved professional success by possessing a number of skills essential for their profession. Of course, they must be creative and passionate about food and eager to continue trying new recipes and creating new dishes. They also must be personable and good leaders because high-level chefs are in charge of all kitchen staff. For that same reason, they need exceptional communication skills, including the ability to listen. They must be honest and professional and able to remain calm in the midst of chaos. And they must have physical stamina because chefs often work long hours standing on their feet. Also essential, says chef Dee Buizer on the Tucson Foodie website, is the ability to not get defensive when criticized. "You need to have *thick skin*—be able to hear criticism even when the guests are wrong or being unreasonable."

On the Job

Employers

According to the US Bureau of Labor Statistics (BLS), chefs and head cooks in the United States held 146,500 jobs during 2016. More than half of their employers were restaurants and other eating establishments. The remainder were employed by special food services, such as food service contractors, caterers, and mobile food services; the traveler accommodation sector, including lodging or short-term accommodations for travelers; and amusement, gambling, and recreation industries.

Working Conditions

As much as chefs often love what they do, it is no secret that their work is hard, the hours are long, and the hazards are plenty. In an article on the Muse career website, Elliott Bell, a graduate of the

Chefs chop vegetables in a restaurant kitchen. Head chefs supervise other chefs and plan menus. Other chefs prepare salads, sauces, and finished plates. All must be adept with knives and other tools of the trade.

French Culinary Institute, writes that "everything about a professional kitchen . . . is easily 100 times more intense than your home kitchen. Knives are sharper, stoves are hotter, space is tighter, and everything moves at a sprint-like pace. Even simple tasks like turning on a stove are much more difficult, and you'll be expected to figure everything out very quickly." Because of the many hazards in commercial kitchens, chefs have a high rate of on-the-job injuries. To reduce risks, chefs typically wear long-sleeve shirts and a chef's coat (even in the heat of summer) and nonslip shoes.

Earnings

Salaries for chefs can vary widely based on years of experience, proven talent, and reputation. According to the BLS, the typical chef's salary ranges from $25,000 to more than $78,500. The website Salary.com cites a higher range, from $57,631 to $81,782.

Opportunities for Advancement

One look at the American Culinary Federation's certifications shows how much room there is for chefs to grow in their careers. The federation offers sixteen different certification levels, from a certified fundamentals cook to a certified master chef. For aspiring chefs who are willing to work hard (no matter how many hours that takes), maintain a positive attitude, absorb all the knowledge they can, deal with the fast pace, and continue to learn and grow, there is virtually no limit to what they can achieve in their careers.

What Is the Future Outlook for Chefs?

Research shows that the future looks good for aspiring chefs. The BLS projects that employment of chefs and head cooks will grow by 10 percent through 2026. That means more than fourteen thousand new jobs will be available in the coming years. In the Tucson Foodie website article, Buizer offers this advice to aspiring chefs: "Follow your passion, be creative, and work hard, and you too will enjoy being a chef as much as I do."

Find Out More

American Culinary Federation
180 Center Place Way
St. Augustine, FL 32095
website: www.acfchefs.org

The American Culinary Federation is the largest professional culinary organization in North America. Its website is an excellent resource for aspiring chefs, with a wealth of information about culinary education, which schools are accredited, a variety of news releases, job updates, and a resource section that offers everything from trends and techniques to recipes.

American Personal & Private Chef Association
4572 Delaware St.
San Diego, CA 92116
website: www.personalchef.com

The American Personal & Private Chef Association supports chefs who are interested in working for private individuals and entities rather than restaurants. Its website provides information on the difference between personal and private chefs, how they get started, links to online study courses, and member forums.

Fresh Chefs Society
5416 Parkcrest Dr., Suite 700
Austin, TX 78731
website: https://freshchefssociety.org

The Fresh Chefs Society is committed to helping young people who are transitioning out of foster care by providing them with culinary skills and educational experiences through exposure to community chefs and restaurants. Its website offers information of interest to aspiring chefs and offers them opportunities to volunteer in their communities.

Future Chefs
560 Albany St.
Boston, MA 02118
website: https://futurechefs.net

As its name implies, Future Chefs is dedicated to young people interested in training to become chefs or other culinary professionals. Its website offers news articles, Future Chefs programs, explanations of how the group's work benefits youth in the Boston community, and links to its newsletter and blog.

James Beard Foundation
167 W. Twelfth St.
New York, NY 10011
website: www.jamesbeard.org

The James Beard Foundation is a culinary arts organization named in honor of the late James Beard, who was a prolific food writer, teacher, and cookbook author. Its website offers a wealth of information for aspiring chefs, including a search engine that produces a variety of culinary-focused articles.

Caterer

Caterers are specialty chefs who are hired by clients to provide food and beverages for special events. These events may be small and intimate affairs, such as a holiday party, bridal shower, or bar/bat mitzvah. Or the events may be large and elaborate, like a community fund-raiser for charity, a high-society wedding reception, or an international business conference. Whatever the occasion, caterers are in charge of every food-related detail, from initial menu planning and selection to tear down and cleanup after an event has ended.

Caterers may work for companies that specialize in catering, event planning firms, hotels, conference centers, or restaurants. Many are self-employed and run their own catering operations. One of these is Tiffany Williams of Chicago, who founded a business called Exquisite Catering & Events. Williams, who is widely known as "Chef Mama," has catered most every type and size of event, from President Barack Obama's second-term fund-raiser to the backstage services at the Lollapalooza summer festival in Chicago.

At a Glance

Caterer

Minimum Educational Requirements
None

Personal Qualities
Excellent cooking skills; ability to plan and prepare a wide variety of foods and meals; good interpersonal, communication, and organizational skills

Certification and Licensing
Sanitary cooking certification by a local board of health

Working Conditions
Indoors or outdoors, depending on the occasion or event being catered

Salary Range
$30,988 to $90,000

Number of Jobs
About 197,000 in May 2017*

Future Job Outlook
Growth of 10 percent through 2026*

*Includes all chef jobs

16

Whether they run their own businesses or work for someone else, caterers have a wide variety of responsibilities. When they are hired to cater an event, caterers meet with the clients and ask all sorts of questions. These cover issues such as what sort of affair it will be (a company picnic? A glitzy formal gala?), the desired date and time, approximately how many people will be invited, and where the event will be held. Another issue discussed at the meeting is the menu. Caterers known for a particular specialty (like Cajun or Mexican food) often have a fixed menu. Others, like caterer Jaclyn Trimble of Rochester, Wisconsin, offer a wider variety of choices and customizable menus. In a January 2018 article in the *Milwaukee Journal Sentinel* newspaper, Trimble shared her thoughts about creating a menu. "I want to know things you like and don't like," she said. "I create the menu around that. . . . Every menu is different." Cost is also discussed at the meeting, particularly whether the client has a budget in mind and, if so, whether it is sufficient to pay for the type of event he or she wants to have. Often this leads to a discussion about how to tailor the desired festivities to better fit the client's budget.

Once all the details of an event have been ironed out and the budget finalized, caterers can get to work. They create menus, figure out exactly what ingredients will be needed, and order and purchase food. "I do all the shopping myself," said Trimble in the 2018 article. Because she wants produce that is fresh and locally grown, she buys it from area farms. "Farmers are my first choice." After the food is prepared, caterers transport it to the event site, being extremely careful to keep hot foods hot and cold foods chilled. Once they have arrived at the site, they unload everything and start setting up. At formal events, servers hired by the caterers will deliver meals to the tables course by course, much like in a restaurant. More casual events often have meals served buffet style, with guests helping themselves to food.

After an event has ended, caterers (often assisted by temporary contract workers) clean up the dining area. Linens are removed from tables, as are plates, dishes, silverware, and glasses. Tables and chairs are taken away, and garbage is cleaned up. Serving equipment and other items belonging to the caterers are returned to the home location. The last step in the process is billing the client for catering services.

Catering can be a high-pressure, high-stress job, and it takes hard work and dedication to succeed. But as far as Trimble is concerned, there is nothing she would rather be doing. In the *Journal Sentinel* article, she commented, "I'm never going to be a millionaire doing this, but I'm going to live a good life because I love what I do."

How Do You Become a Caterer?

Education

There are no educational requirements for becoming a caterer. For those who seek internships, however, an associate's or bachelor's degree in the culinary arts or a related field may be required. Many aspiring caterers previously worked as chefs or earned a degree from an accredited culinary program, so they have extensive knowledge of and training in the culinary arts. Aspiring caterers who want to work for themselves would benefit from taking classes in business management, entrepreneurship, finance, and accounting.

Certification and Licensing

In order to prepare and sell food to the public, caterers must be inspected and certified by their state or local board of health. Requirements for certification vary from locale to locale. Those who want to start their own businesses will need to check with local government offices about necessary licenses or permits.

Although it is not required, the National Association for Catering and Events (NACE) offers a certified professional in catering and events (CPCE) certification. Applicants must complete thirty hours of professional development courses. After study and preparation, they must take a comprehensive CPCE exam that covers accounting, beverage management, catering services, contracts and agreements, event management, food production, human resources, and sales and marketing. The exam includes 175 questions and must be completed in 2.5 hours. Those who pass with a score of 70 percent or greater earn the CPCE designation.

Internships and Volunteer Work

Aspiring caterers would benefit from joining culinary organizations, such as their local branch of NACE. They can get to know catering and events professionals and learn about ways they can volunteer in their communities. On the Muse career website, Jennifer Carver, an events director at the University of Southern California, offers this advice for aspiring event planners, which is a career closely related to catering: "Even if you work in a completely different field, you can volunteer with a local nonprofit and help to plan a fundraising event, or offer to help coordinate an outing or holiday party for your company. Gaining experience will also give you a better perspective of what it takes to plan an event from start to finish and be sure it's really something you want to do."

Involvement with such organizations can also help aspiring caterers become aware of internship opportunities. Internships are often paid (but not always), and they provide valuable hands-on experience. For example, in January 2019 the Park City, Utah, hospitality group Montage International advertised for a catering and conference services intern. The intern would be assisting senior members with a variety of tasks involved with catering, from preplanning event sessions to assisting with catering the event and working with clients.

Skills and Personality

Caterers work with the public, both in trying to build their business and when catering events. So, they need outgoing personalities and excellent interpersonal skills, along with being superb communicators (and listeners). Excellent planning and organizational skills are an absolute must. Caterers are typically under pressure to keep on schedule and meet deadlines, so being able to juggle a seemingly impossible number of tasks—while remaining cool and calm under pressure—is necessary.

Employers

According to the career site Sokanu, there are three types of caterers: mobile caterers, hotel/restaurant caterers, and private caterers. Mobile caterers operate trailers or kiosks in mobile locations like fairs or festivals or in shopping malls. These caterers may hire people for full-time work or on a contract, as-needed basis. Hotel/restaurant caterers handle events and banquets for clients, and they hire their own staffs of catering professionals. Private caterers are those who have earned enough experience and credibility to open their own businesses. Many aspiring caterers dream of someday being self-employed.

Working Conditions

Caterers may work indoors or outdoors, depending on what sort of event they are catering. While preparing the food, they work in commercial kitchens. Working conditions in these kitchens often vary based on the type and size of the facility and due to local laws that govern food service operations. The work environment can be challenging, as an article on the ChefsWorld website explains: "Workers usually must withstand the pressure and strain of standing for hours at a time, lifting heavy pots and kettles, and working near hot ovens and grills. Job hazards include slips and falls, cuts, and burns, but injuries are seldom serious."

While catering events, the workplace might be an office building, a golf course, a wedding reception hall, or even the home of a private client.

Earnings

Caterer earnings vary considerably based on factors such as the size and budget of an event and the caterer's reputation and years of experience. The salary-specific job website Salary.com lists several different levels of caterer salaries. The top earners are catering directors, who make $38,000 to $90,000 per year. Catering managers typically earn $39,973 to more than $55,900, and catering coordinators (entry-level positions) earn $30,988 to $44,111 per year.

Opportunities for Advancement

Caterers can move up the career ladder as they gain more experience, being promoted from an assistant or coordinator to manager or director. Once they have established themselves and built a good reputation, they may decide to open their own businesses. They should proceed with caution, however, since about half of new catering operations go out of business within eighteen months.

What Is the Future Outlook for Caterers?

The National Federation of Independent Business reports that the US catering industry generates more than $8 billion a year. Much of this is from catered events, such as weddings, corporate functions, funerals, holiday parties, and others. Obviously, with $8 billion in sales, there are numerous and varied opportunities for those who want to work in catering.

The US Bureau of Labor Statistics (BLS) does not publicize employment data specifically about caterers, but the projected growth rate for chefs (the closest category to caterer) is 10 percent through 2026. That amounts to 19,700 new jobs. Market forecasts indicate that the catering industry as a whole will achieve healthy growth in the coming years, which is good news for those who dream of becoming caterers. "Catering is an exciting business. You either love it and thrive in it or you don't," said caterer Renee Miner in a September 2018 *Indianapolis Business Journal* article. For her, the job is a perfect fit: "It's definitely in my blood."

Find Out More

American Culinary Federation
180 Center Place Way
St. Augustine, FL 32095
website: www.acfchefs.org

The American Culinary Federation is the largest professional culinary organization in North America. Its website is an excellent resource for anyone who wants to pursue a culinary career, offering information about education, which schools are accredited, news releases, job updates, and a resource section that offers everything from trends and techniques to recipes.

Association of Club Catering Professionals
PO Box 800266
Santa Clarita, CA 91380
website: www.theaccp.com

The Association of Club Catering Professionals seeks to create a community of professionals who specialize in catering to the club industry, meaning yacht clubs, country clubs, and other private establishments. Its website offers information about education, training, and career opportunities.

International Caterers Association
3601 East Joppa Rd.
Baltimore, MD 21234
website: www.internationalcaterers.org

The International Caterers Association provides educational opportunities for catering professionals and those interested in catering careers. Its website provides news articles, opportunities to connect with other catering professionals, and information about upcoming events.

National Association for Catering and Events
10440 Little Patuxent Pkwy., Suite 300
Columbia, MD 21044
website: www.nace.net

With forty chapters throughout the United States, the National Association for Catering and Events provides education, resources, and networking opportunities for catering and event professionals. The "Essential Resources" section of its website contains a great deal of information for anyone interested in a catering career or those who are currently working as caterers.

Brewmaster

What Does a Brewmaster Do?

A brewmaster is someone who makes beer for a living—but not just any beer. Brewmasters, who may also be called head brewers or craft brewers, create their own specialty types of craft beer. These beers are very different from mass-produced brands of beer like Budweiser, Miller, Heineken, and others. "The hallmark of craft beer and craft brewers is innovation," says the Brewers Association on its website. "Craft brewers interpret historic styles with unique twists and develop new styles that have no precedent." The association goes on to explain that brewmasters create their craft beers using traditional ingredients like malted barley. "Interesting and sometimes non-traditional ingredients are often added for distinctiveness." Brewmasters may work at brewing facilities (breweries) or in establishments known as brewpubs. These pubs are owned by a brewery and serve their beer directly to customers.

Brewmasters have many tasks and responsibilities, and their most important goal is to ensure the quality of the beer they are brewing. A brewmaster creates a recipe for his or her own unique beer and then obtains the needed ingredients.

At a Glance

Brewmaster

Minimum Educational Requirements
Bachelor's degree

Personal Qualities
Critical-thinking skills; a passion for the craft; scientific knowledge; decision-making skills

Working Conditions
Inside brewing facilities, which tend to be very warm and often hazardous

Salary Range
$33,941 to 72,019

Number of Jobs
135,072 in 2017*

Future Job Outlook
Projected growth of 6 percent

*Includes all brewery and brewpub jobs

Water, which accounts for about 90 percent of beer's volume, is the main ingredient. On the website 52 Brews, a craft brewer named Mark writes, "When a brewery is thinking about beer making ingredients, a great deal of emphasis is placed on water. While not all beer tastes the same across the board, it's essential that beer of the same brand remains consistent. The role of water is central to this consistency."

Along with water, three other ingredients are essential for making craft beer. These include barley, a cereal grain; hops, which are the flowers of the hop (*Humulus lupulus*) plant that give beer its signature bitter flavor; and yeast, which is required for the fermentation process in which sugar is converted into alcohol. Brewmasters may also add other ingredients, depending on the taste they want to achieve with their craft beer. Some add fruits like peaches, apricots, raspberries, or cherries, as well as cloves or other spices.

The brewing itself is an intricate and complex process that involves a combination of mixing, boiling, waiting, fermenting, cooling—and more waiting. Brewmasters are usually present during most or all of the brewing process. They check temperatures and quality of samples, conduct tests, confer with laboratory staff, and make any necessary adjustments to equipment or procedures to correct any identified problems. They also spend a lot of time watching the clock because proper timing is crucial in beer making.

Throughout every step of the brewing process, it is essential that the brewing equipment be kept clean and sanitized. In fact, brewmasters spend as much time cleaning as on the actual beer making. Contamination can be disastrous, disrupting proper fermentation and ruining an entire batch of beer. "Brewing beer is like being a glorified janitor," quipped Jamie Floyd, a brewmaster in Eugene, Oregon, in a January 2017 article in the British newspaper the *Independent*. "We clean, scrub, rinse and [sanitize] just about everything."

In addition to beer making and cleaning tasks, brewmasters have administrative work. They review the upcoming brewing schedule to determine when ingredients need to be ordered and what quantity is needed. Depending on the size of the brewery, they may have ongoing supervision responsibilities. They are often involved in marketing and promotion of their products, and they maintain relationships with suppliers and vendors.

When thinking about craft beers and the brewmasters who make them, beer enthusiasts are likely to view the job as the ideal occupation. Many brewmasters would agree with that, but they also emphasize that their job is about a lot more than just enjoying their beverages. What they do for a living is equal parts creativity and chemistry, and it requires a great deal of knowledge and precision. Also, the work can be tough, as brewmaster and craft brewery owner Dustin Hazer explained in a February 2018 interview on *Food & Wine* magazine's website: "It is physically demanding work with long hours and typically lower compensation. . . . It is not for everyone, but if and when you find out it is your calling, you will know that it is undoubtedly worth it."

How Do You Become a Brewmaster?

Education

Brewmasters typically have at least a bachelor's degree in chemistry, microbiology, or another branch of science. Some colleges offer specialized degree programs, such as Metropolitan State University in Denver, Colorado, which has four-year degrees in brewery operations and brewpub operations as well as a minor in brewing science. Appalachian State University in Boone, North Carolina, offers a four-year bachelor of science in fermentation science and five-day brewing short courses during the summer months.

Many other schools around the country offer shorter programs that afford aspiring brewmasters the opportunity to gain knowledge and hands-on experience. In September 2016 Grand Rapids Community College (GRCC) in Michigan opened America's first commercial on-campus brewpub owned by a school and run by students. The brewpub is for students enrolled in GRCC's eight-month-long craft brewing, packaging, and service operations certificate program.

A brewmaster checks the quality of a new batch of beer. A new recipe requires extra scrutiny, but even tried and true recipes require monitoring throughout the brewing process.

Students enrolled in the master brewer program at the Siebel Institute of Technology in Chicago complete a twenty-week program. It is divided into one- to eight-week modules, with each module specializing in a particular area of brewing technology. After completing seven weeks of the program, students travel to the world-renowned brewing academy Doemens in Munich, Germany, where they apply the knowledge they have gained in an actual brewing environment at Doemens. They also gain valuable knowledge from presentations on brewing techniques used in creating authentic German beer styles.

Internships and Volunteer Work

It is important for aspiring brewmasters to get hands-on experience any way they can, such as doing one or more internships. This is often the best way to get their foot in the door of a brewery. They gain on-the-job experience and have a head start toward their chosen career. The University of Vermont in Burlington offers the Next Generation Food Systems Internship Program. Internships are paid, and students spend their time at Queen City Brewery, a local craft brewery, where they gain experience in beer making and also learn about the business side of brewing.

Aspiring brewmasters should also look for opportunities to volunteer. For instance, they can visit local breweries and help with tasks such as keg cleaning, bottling, or canning. In a February 2018 article on the *Food & Wine* website, brewmaster Jamey Adams explained that these breweries are often in need of help. "As a volunteer, you can interact with staff members and network within the industry," said Adams. Also, by performing jobs in a brewery—even the most menial jobs—aspiring brewmasters learn the basics of brewing.

Skills and Personality

The brewing business is not for everyone. Certain skills are essential, such as knowledge of science, an aptitude for chemistry, and a desire to learn. Brewers also need strong critical-thinking skills as well as effective project management and organizational skills. They need to be able to work effectively with others and make good decisions. Of particular importance is a passion for their craft because people in the brewing industry typically do what they do because they love it.

On the Job

Employers

The US Bureau of Labor Statistics (BLS) does not publicize employment data specifically about brewmasters or others employed in the craft brewery field. According to the Brewers Association, there were 6,372 craft breweries and brewpubs in the United States as of 2017. These breweries and brewpubs, the association reports, employed 135,072 people during that same year.

Working Conditions

Brewmaster work schedules differ based on where they work and whether their jobs involve mostly managerial or hands-on supervision of the brewing process. The latter is most often the case, especially in small family-owned breweries where everyone pitches in. Brewery work is typically hard and physically demanding, with lots of cleaning and scrubbing, heavy lifting, and long hours. Craft brewer Josh Gordon says that if it were any other type of work, he would not put up with the negatives of working for a brewery. The reason he tolerates the shortcomings is the passion he has for his job. "It's the craft beer industry, and it's what I want to be doing," he says in an article on the BeerAdvocate website. "It's all totally worth it."

Colin Presby's work environment is rather unusual compared with most brewmasters: he works at the Red Frog Pub & Brewery on the *Carnival Vista* cruise ship. It is one of the world's first cruise ship breweries. Presby accepted the job in March 2016 after answering a Carnival Cruise Line job posting for a "brewmaster at sea" on ProBrewer.com. He makes beer right on the ship, using high-tech brewing equipment and seawater that has been desalinated, meaning the salt has been removed from it. In a February 2018 interview on the website Extra Crispy, Presby said there have been challenges along the way and there are sacrifices, but he really enjoys his job and the environment of the ship. "It's a lifestyle that I wouldn't have necessarily seen myself doing before," he said. "but there are aspects of it that are just wonderfully rewarding and fulfilling."

Earnings

According to the salary website PayScale, the salary range for this career is $33,941 to $72,019. The hiring website ZipRecruiter reports a range of $19,500 to $129,500, but it says that the majority of brewmaster salaries in the United States range from $28,000 to $69,500.

Opportunities for Advancement

As with many occupations, brewmasters often start in lower-level positions and work their way up. They may, for example, initially hire in as a cellar worker, a job that involves washing kegs, changing hoses, and ensuring that everything is in place and ready for brewing to begin. As an entry-level employee gains knowledge and experience, he or she may qualify for a promotion to assistant brewmaster. By this time they have learned most everything there is to know about brewing, and they are respected for their knowledge and expertise. Whether they advance in their careers typically depends on how hard they are willing to work.

What Is the Future Outlook for Brewmasters?

Although the BLS does not provide future projections for brewmaster careers, research shows that the craft beer industry has been growing steadily each year. Between 2016 and 2017, for instance, the number of jobs grew 6 percent, from 128,768 in 2016, to 135,072 in 2017. Industry experts predict that strong growth will continue, which likely means opportunities for aspiring brewmasters.

Find Out More

American Brewers Guild
610 Route 7 South
Middlebury, VT 05753
website: www.abgbrew.com

The American Brewers Guild is a brewing school for those who want to learn about making craft beers. Its website offers information about its educational programs, including the Intensive Brewing Science and Engineering, Craftbrewer's Apprenticeship, Working Brewers, and Grain to Glass programs, among others.

BeerAdvocate
PO Box 520144
Winthrop, MA 02152
website: www.beeradvocate.com

BeerAdvocate is an online resource for anyone interested in craft beer. Its website provides information and articles about the craft brewing industry and education and maintains links to online forums.

Brewers Association
1327 Spruce St.
Boulder, CO 80302
website: www.brewersassociation.org

The Brewers Association is an industry trade group that works to support, promote, and protect small and independent American brewers and the craft beers they create. Aspiring brewmasters will find a great deal of valuable information on the website, including industry facts and statistics, best practices, a huge collection of resources, and detailed information about brewpubs.

Master Brewers Association of the Americas
3340 Pilot Knob Rd.
St. Paul, MN 55121
website: www.mbaa.com

The Master Brewers Association seeks to support and promote the craft brewing and allied industries through the exchange of knowledge and experience. Its website offers information about education, jobs, brewery safety, and other issues of interest to craft brewers.

Restaurant Manager

What Does a Restaurant Manager Do?

Restaurant managers are professionals who possess a unique combination of skills. Along with being passionate about food, they are savvy about business matters and are creative thinkers. They must understand everything there is to know about running a restaurant, from managing budgets and overseeing staff to creating a dining environment that entices customers to return over and over again. In an article on the All Culinary Schools website, Maureen "Mo" Shaw, who has worked in restaurant management for years, describes the type of person who is best suited for this career. "It takes somebody that is completely passionate and excited, who has a love for food and people," she says. "You need financial understanding to write budgets, strategic ability to see the big picture, food and wine knowledge, organization, and flexibility. And lots of stamina!" Shaw emphasizes that focusing on the customer is an absolute must. "We're in the people business," she says. "We're

At a Glance

Restaurant Manager

Minimum Educational Requirements
Associate's degree (Bachelor's degree recommended)

Personal Qualities
Passion for food; excellent interpersonal and leadership skills; conflict-resolution skills; ability to work at a fast pace and handle stress

Certification and Licensing
None required for entry-level positions

Working Conditions
Indoors in restaurants

Salary Range
$29,850 to $90,200*

Number of Jobs
About 308,700 in 2016*

Future Job Outlook
Growth of 9 percent through 2026*

*Includes all food service managers

selling a product that our guests come to enjoy, and hopefully, they'll leave with a memorable experience."

As Shaw's description illustrates, a restaurant manager's job is packed with responsibilities. He or she oversees everything that happens in what is known as the front of the house (FOH), meaning anywhere guests are allowed, such as the lobby, bar, and dining rooms. (The kitchen is typically the chef's domain.) When asked what he spends most of his time doing while at work, a restaurant manager named Edward says he plans and prepares the restaurant for guests. In an article on the LifeHacker website, Edward describes this preparation as "mind-boggling." In the hours before the restaurant opens, he makes sure that maintenance staff thoroughly clean it, from the kitchen and restrooms to the dining room and lobby. Tables must be arranged and set up for guests, supply inventories must be checked and verified, and the staff schedule reviewed and approved—no detail can be overlooked.

An extraordinarily important task of a restaurant manager is overseeing staff. This includes interviewing, hiring, training, scheduling, and supervising all FOH employees, including the maître d', hosts and hostesses, servers, bartenders, and busing staff. These are the people who have the most interaction with guests, and the way they do their jobs, including their attitudes, can directly affect how guests feel about the restaurant—and how they talk about it to others. To ensure that employees provide excellent service, the manager must create an environment of positivity, in which employees feel valued and appreciated. This has not always been the norm, says Marie Petulla, who owns and manages two restaurants in Southern California. In a January 2018 article on the American Express website, Petulla explained: "The style of a screaming chef, or screaming manager for that matter, is gone. I think about the way I was brought up in restaurants . . . you can't do that anymore. There is a new generation of workers and they don't respond to that type of behavior."

Another aspect of a restaurant manager's job is to fill in when help is needed. This is especially true when the restaurant is busiest, such as during the lunch or dinner rush. Managers may take orders, carry food from the kitchen to serve guests, refill water glasses, and even bus tables if necessary. For Kasha Walters, the general manager of the popular Hound restaurant in Auburn, Alabama, there is no question that she should pitch in to help. "I'll wash dishes, bus tables, all the way up to forecasting to budgeting for the year to come," Walters says in an online *Auburn Plainsman* article. "Whatever falls into that job description is my responsibility to help ensure that it happens."

No matter where they work, a perspective that restaurant managers overwhelmingly share is that their jobs are not easy. The hours are long, the work can be stressful, and there is a never-ending stream of details to monitor. Employees are sometimes difficult and unreliable, and customers are not always pleasant, even with the best efforts to serve them. Despite the drawbacks, however, those who have a passion for the restaurant business would not want a different career. "Yeah, some nights suck," says Edward in the LifeHacker article, "but if you maintain a great attitude and that attitude spreads to the people around you, you'll have some fun along the way. You can't fake passion. If you have a passion, follow it wherever it takes you."

How Do You Become a Restaurant Manager?

Education

Educational requirements vary in the restaurant business, but most restaurant managers have some postsecondary education: an associate's or bachelor's degree in hospitality management or food service management is common. Such programs typically include coursework in customer service, budgeting and cost estimation, marketing, food service sanitation, and human resources, among others. Newly hired restaurant managers who work for large national chains are typically required to complete their company's specialized training programs.

What is essential for restaurant managers is on-the-job training. Typically, these professionals have worked their way up from lower-level positions and have obtained three to five years of experience. This is essential; restaurant managers oversee all FOH employees, so they need to understand everything about how a restaurant works.

Certification and Licensing
Depending on the state in which they work, restaurant managers may be required to pass a food safety exam and earn the food protection manager certificate. Issued by the American National Standards Institute, the certificate designates that the person is knowledgeable about food safety and sanitation. In addition, restaurant managers can earn the National Restaurant Association's food service management professional certification, which shows leadership, knowledge, and commitment to the industry.

Internships and Volunteer Work
Career experts say that unlike in the past, when employers often hired restaurant managers with limited or no experience, most employers now expect candidates to have experience before applying. That is the benefit of internships, which provide aspiring restaurant managers with valuable on-the-job experience. These positions could vary from working as an assistant chef in charge of food preparation (cutting up vegetables, mixing dough for bread) to assisting the restaurant manager with administrative tasks. Even if duties have little or nothing to do with managing a restaurant, interns can still gain valuable work experience.

Aspiring restaurant managers should also look for opportunities to volunteer in their communities. One way is to join professional organizations like the National Restaurant Association, which offers opportunities to learn about the restaurant industry, earn scholarships, and also meet professionals who work in the culinary arts field. Another option is to volunteer at culinary events such as trade shows. When she was a student in culinary school, Lizzie Powell volunteered at the International Chefs Congress trade show for culinary professionals and vendors. In an article on the Institute of Culinary Education's *Diced* blog, Powell writes,

> Not only was I able to assist food vendors with prep work and their products, but I was able to meet such reputa-

ble chefs as Jeff McInnis and Janine Booth of Root and Bone. Plus, I got to listen to lectures from industry leaders, like Dan Barber of Blue Hill at Stone Barns. For me, this conference was the first experience I've had where I was thrown into the thick of the culinary networking world.

Skills and Personality

Restaurant managers constantly interact with the public, so friendliness and excellent interpersonal skills are essential. They are also team leaders, so they need exceptional communication skills—including the ability to listen as well as speak—and leadership skills. They should be organized, detail oriented, and superb at problem solving, and they must have the ability to remain calm when under pressure or faced with challenging customer or employee issues. Also, because they often have to pitch in when the restaurant is shorthanded, restaurant managers need physical stamina and the willingness to do whatever is needed to keep the restaurant running smoothly.

On the Job

Employers

Restaurant managers work for all kinds of establishments, including tiny roadside cafés; elegant five-star gourmet restaurants in major cities; and restaurant chains such as Cheesecake Factory, Texas Roadhouse, Olive Garden, and Applebee's. According to the National Restaurant Association, there are more than 1 million restaurants operating in the United States, with 14.7 million employees.

Working Conditions

Most restaurant managers work full time, and they typically work more than forty hours per week. It is not unusual for these professionals to work very long days, evenings, and weekends, and sometimes even holidays. Although most of their time is spent in areas frequented by customers, they also visit the kitchen. This is typically a crowded, very busy (sometimes chaotic) area that has a number of hazards, including hot ovens, hot pans on the stove, and slippery floors. As a result, says the US Bureau of Labor Statistics (BLS), restaurant managers have a higher rate of injuries than most occupations.

Earnings

The BLS estimates that annual salaries for food service managers range from $29,850 to more than $90,200. Salaries for restaurant managers can vary widely based on education, certification, skills, years of experience, and the type of restaurant and its location. In a December 2018 article on the Balance career website, veteran restaurateur Lorri Mealey wrote, "Managing a five-star restaurant in New York City can bring in as much as six figures. Managing a chain restaurant . . . offers around $50,000 a year, with benefits."

Opportunities for Advancement

The National Restaurant Association reports that eight out of nine restaurant managers start their careers as entry-level employees. As they gain experience, credibility, and knowledge, they move up the career ladder. According to an October 2018 article on the website for *Restaurant Insider* magazine,

> While starting at entry level can be difficult, the best managers know and understand every facet of their restaurant, including how the meals get made to how the guests are seated. Plus, managers are often tasked with jumping into various roles—everything from prepping to bartending—on busy nights. The best ones become that way by truly knowing how to do it all.

Since managers hold the top positions in restaurants, they have two options for career advancement: to change jobs for a more prestigious management position or move into restaurant ownership. Those who choose the latter often still function as managers so they can maintain close control over their business interests and reputations.

What Is the Future Outlook for Restaurant Managers?

The BLS estimates that food service manager jobs will grow 9 percent through 2026, which amounts to 27,600 new jobs. According to the National Restaurant Association, the future looks bright for the restaurant industry and those who aspire to become a part of it, as its website states: "If you're looking for a job in the restaurant industry, you've made a smart choice. The restaurant industry is the second largest private-sector employer in the United States, and it adds jobs at a stronger rate than all other industries combined." As the restaurant industry continues to grow, the need for skilled restaurant managers will inevitably grow as well.

Find Out More

American Culinary Federation
180 Center Place Way
St. Augustine, FL 32095
website: www.acfchefs.org

The American Culinary Federation seeks to promote a professional image of American culinary professionals worldwide. Its website is primarily targeted at chefs and others who work in traditional culinary careers, but it offers a great deal of information about the culinary industry that would be of interest to restaurant managers.

International Association of Culinary Professionals
45 Rockefeller Plaza, Suite 2000
New York, NY 10111
website: www.iacp.com

The International Association of Culinary Professionals is a non-profit organization whose members work in culinary education, communication, and the preparation of food and beverages. Its website provides information of interest to restaurant managers, especially its blog, which has articles on a wide variety of culinary-related topics.

National Restaurant Association
2055 L St. NW, Suite 700
Washington, DC 20036
website: https://restaurant.org

The National Restaurant Association is the world's largest food service trade association, supporting more than five hundred thousand restaurant businesses. Its website offers news articles, industry research and statistics, information about restaurant careers, and much more.

Society for Hospitality and Foodservice Management
326 E. Main St.
Louisville, KY 40202
website: www.shfm-online.org

The Society for Hospitality and Foodservice Management exists to support executives in the corporate food service and workplace hospitality industries. Its website offers career information, news articles, an online newsletter, and information about the Young Professional Rising Star Scholarship Program.

Food Stylist

What Does a Food Stylist Do?

Whenever people admire—even drool over—gorgeous food photos, they probably have no idea of what went on behind the scenes before the photos were taken. They may not know that someone spent a great deal of time arranging the food to be photographed before the camera started clicking. That "someone" is a food stylist, a professional who specializes in making food look beautiful and appetizing in photographs—which is why food stylists are sometimes called makeup artists for food. In a May 2018 article on the *BBC Good Food* blog, health editor Sarah Lienard wrote, "A food stylist's job is to help create the kind of irresistible images that make you want to lick the page they're printed on."

Food stylists are artists as well as passionate foodies. Their work appears in magazines, ads, cookbooks, and movies as well as on billboards, websites, and television. They often work as independent contractors and are hired on a freelance basis for photo shoots. This is true of Jillian McCann, who owns a business in Chicago, Illinois, called Jillian McCann Food Stylist. McCann started out working as a commercial photo stylist, but she was intrigued by watching food stylists work in a photography studio. "I was drawn to the work they were doing," said McCann in a July 2018 story on the VoyageChicago website. "At some point, it made sense to marry my love of cooking with my skills as a photo stylist." Today, McCann's talent as a food stylist is displayed in print publications, advertisements, catalogs, and videos as well as on shopping websites and food packaging.

When food stylists are hired for a job, they collect all the accessories they will need. This can include tablecloths, placemats, cloth napkins, flatware, plates, and other such items. Unless they are working with a chef who prepares the food, stylists do the cooking themselves. So, after reviewing recipes, they make lists and shop for all the groceries. Food stylist Jennifer Joyce says in a *BBC Good Food* article, "Working as a food stylist you have to know how to cook everything from pastry and a three-layer cake to a joint of meat. There isn't time on a job to start looking things up—you need extensive knowledge about all types of food."

When it is time for a photo shoot to begin, the photo stylist arranges the prepared food artfully on a plate and keeps tweaking it until it looks as attractive and appetizing as possible. Joyce says that some foods are much harder to style and look attractive than others. "Brown and homey foods, such as shepherd's pie, lasagna and stews, are particularly tricky," she says. To compensate for the bland appearance, Joyce sometimes uses raw chopped ingredients or fresh herbs to help brighten up the dishes.

Like all food stylists, Joyce uses an assortment of tools and gadgets in her work. She carries a large toolbox along to all her photo shoots, and it contains every conceivable item that she might need: a potato masher, a variety of knives, a utensil for slicing vegetables known as a mandolin, a zester for scraping the rind (zest) of lemons and oranges, a thermometer, and a peeler. Joyce also carries along a separate bag containing larger items, like a blender, a hand mixer, pastry cutters, and a blow torch. Food stylists often use blow torches to char meat before it is photographed to give it a nicely browned appearance.

Charring meat with a blow torch is one of many tricks stylists use to make food look especially delicious. They sometimes touch food up with paint or dye to enhance its color, stuff a turkey or chicken with paper towels to make it look fatter, and hold food in place with globs of putty or wax. In a January 2016 article on his website, Dantasticfood, food stylist Dan Macey described another food styling trick. "Imagine you're flipping through a food magazine and you see an article on ice cream," he said. "Accompanying the article is a picture that activates your drool glands: A hot-fudge sundae with vanilla ice cream and a cherry on top, served in a frosted glass. You never knew food photography was so good at making your stomach rumble, and you'd like nothing more than to take a bite out of that sundae." That would be a bad idea, however, because what looks like ice cream might actually be a scoop of mashed potatoes. "That sundae is indeed too good to be true," said Macey, "and it's all thanks to a food stylist."

Education

Food stylists should have a minimum of a high school diploma or equivalent, and additional education in the culinary arts is advantageous. Their jobs require them to thoroughly understand food and be accomplished cooks. Joyce urges aspiring food stylists to earn a culinary arts degree: "It's pretty vital to have a cooking qualification from a reputed cooking school. . . . If you assist someone they want to know you can chop, cook and move fast. There are lots of stylists, like me, who are self-taught, but nowadays that's rare."

Internships and Volunteer Work

Only those who fully understand the culinary industry, have on-the-job experience styling food-related photo shoots, and have put together a portfolio of their work can hope to be hired for photo-styling assignments. Thus, aspiring food stylists must do everything possible to gain experience and add to their portfolios. Internships are one way to do that, but they are often available only to college students.

In the interest of gaining experience, aspiring food stylists should seek out volunteer opportunities, such as helping during photo shoots. "The only way to learn and meet clients is to assist other food stylists," says Joyce in her *BBC Good Food* interview. "This usually involves working for free initially for six months and then you move on to paid assisting jobs." Joyce adds that it can take anywhere from six months to a year for food stylists-in-training to start getting their own assignments.

Skills and Personality

In order to make it in the food styling business, aspiring stylists need a unique combination of qualities. They need a passion for food, an artistic eye, and a great imagination. They should have a good understanding of the photographic process and keen attention to detail. Food stylists often cook the food for photo shoots, so they need cooking skills and an overall understanding of the culinary industry. Also needed are organization and interpersonal skills, the ability to work well in teams, and plenty of patience.

On the Job

Employers

Food stylists often work as freelancers and are hired on a project basis by photographers who specialize in food photography. Stylists may also be employed by companies who hire in-house stylists. Some advertising agencies employ food stylists, as do food magazine publishers, cookbook publishers, and larger restaurant chains.

Working Conditions

Food stylists often work odd hours because they must be available whenever photo shoots are scheduled—day or night. They spend many hours on their feet, and bending over to continuously make adjustments to food can be tiring as well as hard on their backs. On the website of the *Des Moines Register* newspaper, food stylist Susan Strelecki comments, "You're exhausted and on your feet, using paintbrushes and tweezers with your face in an oven, spraying a turkey with a secret brew and all under deadline pressure." But, she adds, "still, you love it."

Food stylists typically work in photography studios, where lighting can be carefully controlled. Yet some photo shoots take place on location—in a restaurant or even outside—and stylists must be prepared for the conditions. On these occasions, travel is often necessary and may require overnight stays.

Earnings

According to the salary and benefits website PayScale, the salary range for food stylists is $30,410 to $121,217. Those with the most experience and talent will make the highest amount of money. Geographic location also makes a difference. Generally, photo stylists working in large metropolitan areas will earn the highest wages.

Opportunities for Advancement

Photo styling is a career that is built over time as knowledge, talent, and experience are accumulated. Those who are willing to work hard, work crazy hours, and do whatever sorts of tasks need to be done at a photo shoot are most likely to advance in their careers. Jillian McCann knew she wanted to work in food styling, but she had no experience with that specialty. She spent three years doing food-styling projects on the side, in addition to her regular job, until she was qualified to go on her own. "Work doesn't just come to you," McCann said in her VoyageChicago interview. "You have to go out and find clients in order to build your business." For aspiring food stylists who are willing to put in the time and effort, career advancement is very much within reach.

What Is the Future Outlook for Food Stylists?

Although job information about food stylists is not publicized by the BLS, it projects that jobs for various types of designers will grow by 5 percent through 2026. One thing is certain for food stylists: as long as photographs of food are in demand, stylists will be needed to make those photos look irresistible.

Find Out More

American Culinary Federation
180 Center Place Way
St. Augustine, FL 32095
website: www.acfchefs.org

The American Culinary Federation is the largest professional culinary organization in North America. Its website is an excellent resource for aspiring culinary professionals, including stylists, because it offers so much valuable information about the industry.

American Institute of Wine & Food
26384 Carmel Rancho Ln., Suite 200e
Carmel, CA 93923
website: www.aiwf.org

The American Institute of Wine & Food is a nonprofit organization dedicated to advancing the understanding, appreciation, and quality of wine and food. Aspiring food stylists can learn a great deal about the culinary industry by perusing the various publications available through its website.

American Photographic Artists
5042 Wilshire Blvd., Suite 321
Los Angeles, CA 90036
website: https://apanational.org

American Photographic Artists is a national organization run by and for professional photographers. Numerous articles about food photography are available through the website, which could help aspiring food stylists increase their practical knowledge.

International Association of Culinary Professionals
45 Rockefeller Plaza, Suite 2000
New York City, NY 10111
website: www.iacp.com

The International Association of Culinary Professionals is a non-profit organization whose members work in culinary education, communication, and the preparation of food and beverages. Its website provides information that could be of interest to anyone working in the culinary industry or thinking about a culinary career.

Food Writer

What Does a Food Writer Do?

For someone with a passion for food and a flair for writing, being a food writer could be a natural fit. Food writers contribute to innumerable publications, online as well as in print. These include culinary magazines such as *Saveur*, *Gourmet*, *Bon Appétit*, *Food & Wine*, *Cuisine*, *Fine Cooking*, and *Cook's Illustrated*. Food writers also write culinary-related articles for mainstream publications, including *USA Today*, the *New York Times*, the *New Yorker*, and many others. As food blogs have continued to grow in popularity, many food-loving writers have begun blogging. Food writers also write cookbooks, and in many cases they personally create the recipes that are featured. All in all, the opportunities are many and diverse for those who are interested in a food-writing career. In an article on the Muse career website, food writer Jessica Battilana says, "You won't be able to land your dream food-writing job right out of the gate, but the food industry is a huge, diverse business and there are many things you can do within it."

At a Glance

Food Writer

Minimum Educational Requirements
Bachelor's degree

Personal Qualities
Strong writing and editing skills; passion for and knowledge of food; research skills; critical-thinking skills; flexibility; good interpersonal skills

Certification and Licensing
None

Working Conditions
An office inside or outside the home, or anywhere else there is access to a computer and an Internet connection

Salary Range
$30,520 to $118,760*

Number of Jobs
About 131,200*

Future Job Outlook
Growth of 8 percent through 2026*

*Includes all types of writers

Battilana, who lives in San Francisco, has written for all kinds of publications. Her culinary articles have been featured in *Martha Stewart Living*, the *New York Times*, the *Wall Street Journal*, *Gastronomica*, *Saveur*, *Sunset*, and multiple editions of the book *The Best Food Writing*. She writes a bimonthly column for the *San Francisco Chronicle* called *Repertoire: All the Recipes You Need*, and in 2018 she published a cookbook by the same name. In addition to writing the text, she developed all the recipes featured in the book.

Battilana's cookbook-writing process, as she describes in an interview on the Marketplace website, begins with grocery shopping for ingredients. "If I'm lucky, I go to the grocery store just once," she says. "But often it's a couple trips to the grocery store or trips to a few different stores to get a few different things." Once she has all the ingredients, Battilana begins to cook whatever it is that she has envisioned. This may involve cooking the same dish over and over again. As she explains in the interview, "Sometimes it's amazing and things work on the first or second try, and sometimes they don't. Sometimes it takes 10 or 15 tries to get a recipe the way you want it." During and after the cooking, Battilana jots down notes about what went right and wrong and how long the dish has taken to cook. Those notes are used to write her recipes, and then all the information is put together in a cookbook.

When a food writer has been assigned an article for print or online publications (including blogs), the process begins with research (information gathering). The type of research and where it is obtained will depend on the writing assignment. If the assignment is a restaurant review, for example, the writer will visit the restaurant, interview the manager and the chef, order a meal, and take detailed notes. If the subject matter is a city's farmers market and the farm-fresh produce that is available there, the writer will visit these markets and interview a variety of people, from farmers to customers and workers. For an article about the heritage of a particular type of food, the writer may conduct research on the Internet, use historical documents, and conduct interviews in person, on the phone, or through video chat technology.

Food blogs have vastly expanded opportunities for all kinds of writers, including those who want to write about food. One of these bloggers is Helen Fletcher of St. Louis, Missouri, whose blog is called *Pastries Like a Pro*. Fletcher, who owned an upscale bakery for twenty-five years, is now a pastry chef at a high-end restaurant. Through her years of experience she has developed a number of techniques for master baking. She shares these techniques, along with recipes, tips, and ideas. "My blog reflects my love of what I do, the creativity involved and writing," Fletcher explained in a 2017 online article about food bloggers. She has been delighted at the positive response from visitors to her blog. "I am constantly surprised at my readers thanking me for sharing my recipes and knowledge," she said.

How Do You Become a Food Writer?

Education

Writers of all specialties, including those whose passion and focus is food, generally need to earn a bachelor's degree in English, journalism, marketing, or communications. Classes in creative writing are also valuable. Aspiring food writers can also benefit from taking classes in the culinary arts so they can learn as much as possible about food and the culinary industry. Another option is taking online food-writing courses, which can help aspiring food writers learn more about the writing techniques they will need to master in order to become professional writers.

Raquel Pelzel, who is senior food writer for the food and beverage group Tasting Table, was a college student participating in a copywriting internship when it occurred to her that she wanted a food-related career. She enrolled in a vegetarian cooking school in Colorado. After a few years of writing for various publications, she enrolled in culinary school to study pastry making. In an interview on the Muse website, she explains how all this study led to her career as a food writer. "I kind of put my love of writing together with my love of food," Pelzel says. She heard about a job opening at the food magazine *Cook's Illustrated* and decided she had nothing to lose by applying. She was hired as a food writer and says that experience really launched her career.

Internships and Volunteer Work

Because writing experience is essential for aspiring food writers, they should take advantage of any opportunities to gain that experience. For Pelzel, the internship is what opened her eyes to what she really wanted to do for her career—and what she did not want to do (copywriting). Internships can also provide aspiring food writers with valuable work experience.

Young people who want careers in food writing should seek out opportunities to volunteer. For instance, they might offer to write a newsletter or other materials for a local food bank, farmers market, charity, or restaurant. They can also volunteer to write for these and other organizations' websites. Another excellent way to gain food-writing experience and become a better writer is by creating a food blog. By researching and writing interesting articles about food, aspiring food writers can build a group of followers and also connect with other food writers by following their blogs.

Skills and Personality

Along with excellent writing skills, food writers must be very good at research and know how to find information when they need it. They need superb communication skills, especially the ability to listen well, and also interviewing skills. They must be determined and not easily discouraged, which requires patience and adaptability. Also important is the ability to take criticism well because they will undoubtedly work for publishers and editors who will critique their work and sometimes find fault with it.

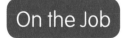

On the Job

Employers

Food writers often work as freelancers, but others are employed by major magazines or publishers. They may also work for advertising agencies that specialize in the food industry or for large restaurant chains that have their own creative staffs. Those who are freelance writers work on a contract basis for a wide variety of cookbook publishers and food publications. According to the US Bureau of Labor Statistics (BLS), 64 percent of all writers and authors are self-employed.

Working Conditions

Food writers typically work in an office in their home or at another location, wherever they have access to a computer and an Internet connection. Their work schedules can vary widely based on deadlines, especially for freelancers. It is not uncommon for food writers to get rush projects and have to work nights and weekends to meet tight deadlines.

Earnings

The BLS reports that annual salaries for writers and authors range from $30,520 to $118,760. According to the salary and benefits website PayScale, the average pay for a food editor is $50,868 per year.

Opportunities for Advancement

Everyone has to start somewhere, and aspiring food writers who are fiercely motivated to succeed and willing to work hard to get there will undoubtedly make it. In an article on her blog, *Sandra's Kitchen Studio*, accomplished food writer and cookbook author Sandra A. Gutierrez offers some advice for aspiring food writers: "First, you've got to write; second, you've got to know food. Then, like everyone else in this business, you'll need to build your way up to getting your first piece published, and so on. Each step is necessary in order to learn the craft. . . . More importantly, as with any job, you need to be passionate about the work—after all, professional food writing is a job."

What Is the Future Outlook for Food Writers?

The BLS offers a promising outlook for writers in the coming years. It projects 8 percent growth through 2026, which amounts to about ten thousand new jobs for writers of all types.

Some people are cynical about the future for food writers, saying that opportunities to make a living are diminishing. In an article on the restaurant website Eater, editor in chief Amanda Kludt makes it clear that there are plenty of opportunities for food writers to acquire paying work. She writes,

> You can now find (paid) food writing in the *New Yorker*, the *New York Times* (and its magazines), the *Wall Street Journal* (and its magazine), men's mags, [food magazines] . . . , and others, not to mention regional and local out-fits. All of these publications pay writers. Eater manages to pay dozens of full-time writer/editor salaries, plus a bevy of freelancers.

Find Out More

American Institute of Wine & Food
26384 Carmel Rancho Ln., Suite 200e
Carmel, CA 93923
website: www.aiwf.org

The American Institute of Wine & Food is a nonprofit organization dedicated to advancing the understanding, appreciation, and quality of wine and food. Aspiring food writers could find it valuable to peruse the many publications available through its website.

Association of Food Journalists
2190 W. Alameda St., Apt. B
Santa Fe, NM 87507
website: www.afjonline.com

The Association of Food Journalists is dedicated to helping its members adapt to and excel in the rapidly changing field of food journalism. Its website offers articles about the culinary industry that aspiring food writers might find helpful, although access to the full site requires membership.

International Association of Culinary Professionals
45 Rockefeller Plaza, Suite 2000
New York, NY 10111
website: www.iacp.com

The International Association of Culinary Professionals is a non-profit organization whose members work in culinary education, communication, and the preparation of food and beverages. Its website provides information that could be of interest to anyone working in the culinary industry or thinking about a culinary career.

International Food, Wine & Travel Writers Association
39252 Winchester Rd., Suite 107, #418
Murrieta, CA 92563
website: www.ifwtwa.org

The International Food, Wine & Travel Writers Association is a network of food, wine, and travel journalists and the people who promote them. Aspiring food writers can find a variety of interesting materials on its website, including articles written by members, several different online magazines, and general information about food writing.

Pastry Chef

What Does a Pastry Chef Do?

Pastry chefs are specialty chefs who exhibit their artistry through the creation of desserts and baked goods. An astounding array of layer cakes, pies, tarts, soufflés, and gourmet chocolates are created by pastry chefs, as are artisan breads, homemade pretzels, and gourmet snacks. They often have the creative freedom to experiment with recipes and introduce their own custom-made creations. For Sarah Kelso, who is the pastry chef at Bon Appétit Restaurant in Dunedin, Florida, customers provide the inspiration for the desserts she creates. She spoke about this in a November 2017 interview on the restaurant's website. "I try to think of what our customers will enjoy most," she said. "I'll test something for a few weeks and ask the servers for feedback."

Kelso also chooses her desserts based on the season. During the summer months, she opts for desserts that are light and refreshing, often choosing ingredients that she can get locally. When the weather gets cooler, Kelso's desserts start

At a Glance

Pastry Chef

Minimum Educational Requirements
High school diploma or equivalent

Personal Qualities
Creativity and imagination; keen attention to detail; communication skills; math ability; physical stamina and strength

Certification and Licensing
Certification not required for entry-level positions

Working Conditions
A variety of culinary environments, including kitchens in restaurants, hotels, resorts, or other establishments, and in bakeries

Salary Range
$25,020 to $78,570*

Number of Jobs
About 146,500 in 2016*

Future Job Outlook
Growth of 10 percent through 2026*

*includes all types of chefs

getting a little heavier. Her sweet potato pie with streusel topping, for instance, is a huge hit with restaurant guests. "Oh, it's delicious," commented Kelso. "Each bite offers the perfect mix of creaminess and crunch with hints of citrus and spice. The top is a tasty crumble made up of pecans, brown sugar, cinnamon and sea salt. Guests can't stop raving about it!" Other mouthwatering desserts Kelso created include a European-style cheesecake with strawberry sauce and a vanilla-cinnamon crust and an apple-cranberry tart served warm with vanilla bean ice cream.

Pastry chefs like Kelso are typically on the job very early in the morning, sometimes hours before the rest of the kitchen staff arrive. This is just part of the job, and pastry chefs learn to accept it. In fact, once they get used to waking up before dawn (which takes some time), many learn to like the early hours. The kitchen is quieter then, absent the usual hustle and bustle of meal preparation, and there is more room for the pastry chefs to work.

New York City pastry chef Melissa Weller usually arrives at work by 5:00 a.m. After looking over the day's tasks, she and her assistant begin the early morning baking, which includes Weller's famous sticky buns. Throughout the morning they mix doughs for soft pretzels and the sweet yeast bread known as babka, which they shape and bake for the lunch offering. They also make Italian flatbread (focaccia), chocolate chip cookies, and chocolate-buckwheat teacakes known as madeleines. In the afternoon, Weller takes care of paperwork, preps all the pastries and breads that will be baked the next morning, and tests recipes, sometimes replacing them if necessary. Weller's day typically ends at about 5:00 p.m., after working a twelve-hour day.

Such long hours are not uncommon for pastry chefs, who work very hard. In the course of a day, it is not unusual for a pastry chef to lug around sacks of flour and sugar that weigh at least 50 pounds (23 kg) and lift enormous mixing bowls that hold 15 pounds (7 kg) of bread dough. In one shift, these chefs might make everything from pizza dough and a three-layer chocolate cake to crème brûlée. Their work moves at a fast pace, and there is not always time for a break. In an April 2016 online *Pittsburgh Post-Gazette* article, pastry chef Amanda Williams insisted, "It's a lot of hard work. It's not like baking at home."

In addition to their prep work and whipping up amazing culinary delicacies, pastry chefs often hire, train, and supervise their assistants and junior pastry chefs. They also take inventory, order supplies, tweak menu items, and ensure that food safety measures are followed and enforced.

Despite the packed schedules, the hard work, and the long days, many pastry chefs love their jobs. This is true of pastry chef Danielle O'Day, who in the summer of 2018 opened her own business, Sweet Dee's Bakeshop in Scottsdale, Arizona. Within just a few months of the opening, eager customers were lining up daily to buy her famous pastries. In an August 2018 interview with *Forbes* magazine published online, O'Day said she was thrilled that her business was succeeding, but she admitted that the hours could be tough: "When they say you don't ever go home from the business that you own, they were right. I've enjoyed every aspect of this wild ride, but a nap always sounds pretty good." Still, O'Day is doing exactly what she wants to do. "I've learned that it never feels like work when you're doing what you love."

How Do You Become a Pastry Chef?

Education

Pastry chefs are not required to have a college degree, but a culinary arts education can be a huge benefit to them. Exact coursework varies from program to program, but topics generally include basic culinary arts skills, cost and inventory control, menu development, food preparation, food safety and sanitation, culinary math, and international cooking. For a specialty in pastry, courses may cover chocolate making, quick breads, yeast breads, baking techniques (both classical and modern), working with crusts, cake decorating, baking for events and competitions, and ice cream and caramels. Kriss Harvey, who is now a well-known pastry chef and chocolatier in Los Angeles, describes his grueling experience with pastry chef training in an article on the *Los Angeles Times* website: "Every day for a year, I was making tart shells a little larger than the size of a nickel over and over

A pastry chef adds the final decorative touches to a wedding cake. Pastry chefs create all sorts of desserts including layer cakes, pies, tarts, and soufflés. Some also make artisan breads and gourmet snacks.

again," says Harvey. "The best pastry chefs know this is how you get good at something. It's like being a body builder. You lift and lift and lift."

What is absolutely essential for aspiring pastry chefs is on-the-job experience. Some are fortunate enough to land apprenticeships or internships and work under established pastry chefs. According to the Art Career Project, real-world experience might be offered as a segment of culinary school classroom work. Also, some schools have restaurants as part of their campus, where students work as they attend school. Creating pastries for restaurant guests provides excellent real-life experience. In Muskegon, Michigan, the Sweet Spot is a downtown restaurant owned and staffed by the Culinary Institute of Michigan. The restaurant sells fresh pastries, breads, cookies, and chocolate specialties, all of which are made by students in the institute's baking and pastry program.

Certification and Licensing

According to the US Bureau of Labor Statistics (BLS), chefs (including pastry chefs) are not required to be certified or licensed.

But several culinary organizations offer certifications for pastry chefs, which can lead to more prestigious positions and higher salaries. The American Society of Baking offers certifications, as do the Institute of Culinary Education and the American Culinary Federation.

Internships and Volunteer Work

Aspiring pastry chefs who attend culinary school will often be required to complete one or more internships. These are often paid (but not always) and can provide aspiring pastry chefs with valuable on-the-job experience that could help them land their first job in a pastry kitchen. Sometimes, aspiring pastry chefs are fortunate enough to do internships in Europe, working under master pastry chefs in France or other countries.

Skills and Personality

It takes individuals of a certain type to succeed as pastry chefs. They must be artistic and passionate about creating pastries and other baked goods. They need excellent interpersonal skills because they often work with and/or supervise other culinary staff. They need patience and keen concentration as well as superb attention to detail. On the website of the Auguste Escoffier School of Culinary Arts, New York City pastry chef Fabian Von Hauske describes how pastry chefs differ from many other culinary professionals: "Most pastry chefs tend to possess an incredibly organized and precise temperament. We're much less about being spontaneous in our cooking, because pastry has to be exact. It's science."

On the Job

Employers

Pastry chefs are employed by restaurants, bakeries, hotels, resorts, country clubs, and even cruise ships. Some own their own businesses or sell their culinary creations to specialty stores; others work as freelance pastry chefs for caterers or restaurants.

They may also work for culinary institutions as instructors for aspiring pastry chefs.

Working Conditions

Working conditions can vary widely depending on where pastry chefs work. But as is customary for those in the culinary industry, pastry chefs often have to work long hours in a kitchen, which can be tough. They stand for long periods while observing the baking process, making huge bowls of dough, and cleaning baking equipment. In the *HuffPost* blog, Lisa Siva describes the unpleasant work environment she endured while working for a famous French pastry chef in the kitchen of a New York City restaurant. "While I've always been happiest in the kitchen," says Siva, "there is nothing quite like standing for hours on end and sweating in the radiant heat of multiple, roaring ovens between shelves of couverture [chocolate] and vanilla beans. The home kitchen is worlds apart from the professional one."

Pastry chefs start their day very early in the morning—sometimes as early as 3:00 or 4:00 a.m. To many people, that may seem undesirable, but some pastry chefs find it appealing. Even though they must start work before dawn, they get to leave for the day while other restaurant employees still have many hours left on their shifts.

Earnings

Pastry chef salaries are based on a number of factors, including years of experience, education and credentials, proven talent, and reputation. According to the BLS, during 2016 chefs of all types earned from $25,020 to more than $78,570. The website Salary.com shows a salary for high-level pastry chefs that ranges from $52,696 to $78,886.

Opportunities for Advancement

As pastry chefs acquire additional skills and years of experience, they can advance in their careers. Many start out as assistants or junior pastry chefs and can move into higher-level positions such as executive pastry chef and master pastry chef. Many find that the best way to advance their careers is to change positions, and changing jobs several times over the course of their career is common.

What Is the Future Outlook for Pastry Chefs?

There are promising signs for pastry chefs in the future. The BLS projects a 10 percent growth in jobs for all chefs through the year 2026. The bureau also provides job information for bakers, and it predicts 8 percent growth through 2026.

Find Out More

AIB International
1213 Bakers Way
Manhattan, KS 66505
website: www.aibonline.org

Formerly the American Institute of Baking, AIB International supports culinary professionals on the baking side of the industry through research and education. Its website links to a *Food First* blog, which offers numerous articles of interest to aspiring pastry chefs.

American Culinary Federation
180 Center Place Way
St. Augustine, FL 32095
website: www.acfchefs.org

The American Culinary Federation is the largest professional culinary organization in North America. Its website is an excellent resource for aspiring chefs of all types, including pastry chefs, with a wealth of information about culinary education. It provides information on which schools are accredited, a variety of news releases, job updates, and a resource section that offers everything from trends and techniques to recipes.

American Society of Baking
7809 N. Chestnut Ave.
Kansas City, MO 64119
website: www.asbe.org

The American Society of Baking is a professional organization whose members are commercial baking professionals, food technologists, and others who are dedicated to advancing baking and baking science technology. Aspiring pastry chefs can find a lot of good industry information on the website, which has sections on baking specialties, food safety, processes, and more.

Pastry Chefs of America
209 S. Bridge St.
Grand Ledge, MI 48837
website: www.pastrychefsofamerica.org

Founded in 1914, Pastry Chefs of America seeks to educate, support, and advocate for professionals in the pastry industry. Aspiring pastry chefs will find a good collection of resources on its website, although membership is required to access most of the material.

Flavorist

What Does a Flavorist Do?

The field of culinary arts is large and diverse, with innumerable career possibilities, both traditional and nontraditional. One of the more nontraditional culinary careers is the flavor chemist, or flavorist, as these professionals are often known. Flavorists are scientists who create new and improved flavors for every conceivable type of food. When new ice cream flavors appear in the supermarket, for instance, flavorists created those flavors. When Nabisco introduced its new lemon-flavored Oreo cookies, that new flavor was created by flavorists. When a child squeals with delight at how yummy a lollipop tastes, that is the work of flavorists. In an October 2017 article on the FoodGrads website, aspiring flavorist Veronica Hislop explained, "A flavourist acts as a magician combining different flavours to create the perfect blend to make a magical treat."

Flavorists develop flavors using a precise combination of chemicals. Some people find this idea to be distasteful, believing that their foods should

At a Glance

Flavorist

Minimum Educational Requirements
Bachelor's degree (chemistry often preferred)

Personal Qualities
Strong critical-thinking, communication, math, and chemistry skills; keen sense of taste and smell; imagination and curiosity

Certification and Licensing
None required for entry-level positions

Working Conditions
In laboratories and occasionally in offices

Salary Range
$37,890 to $116,520*

Number of Jobs
About 17,000 in 2016*

Future Job Outlook
Growth of 6 percent through 2026

*includes all food scientists

be all natural and contain nothing artificial whatsoever. Yet much of this perception is due to being uninformed or misinformed, as scientists say there is very little difference in the chemical compositions of natural and artificial flavorings. Whereas natural flavorings are derived from spices, fruits, vegetables, herbs, or other natural products, artificial flavorings are made in a laboratory. Both types are created by flavorists who blend appropriate chemicals together in exactly the right proportions. In an article on the website of *Scientific American* magazine, food scientist Gary Reineccius writes,

> The flavorist uses "natural" chemicals to make natural flavorings and "synthetic" chemicals to make artificial flavorings. The flavorist creating an artificial flavoring must use the *same* chemicals in his formulation as would be used to make a natural flavoring, however. Otherwise, the flavoring will not have the desired flavor. The distinction in flavorings—natural versus artificial—comes from the *source* of these identical chemicals and may be likened to saying that an apple sold in a gas station is artificial and one sold from a fruit stand is natural.

In the course of their jobs, flavorists have numerous responsibilities and tasks. They work in a laboratory and create new and improved flavors using individual flavor components, such as essential oils, botanical extracts, essences, and synthetic compounds. During the process they must draw on their extensive knowledge of science, combined with their excellent senses of taste and smell. In a September 2017 article on the Society of Flavor Chemists (SFC) website, food scientist Bryan Quoc Le illustrates the process flavorists use with a metaphor, saying that synthesizing a desired flavor is "much like how a pianist must bring together notes to play a song or a perfumer creates a new scent using a multitude of fragrant chemicals."

Le goes on to explain that along with creating new flavors, flavorists must continuously keep up with regulations, the availability and cost of ingredients, culinary trends, and innovations in flavor.

On occasion, flavorists may go on trips to what Le calls "culinary hot spots of the world" in order to gain inspiration for new flavor concepts. Industry organizations also hold study trips to locations around the world, where flavorists can learn about new trends and innovative flavors. "The career of a flavorist is one of constant learning, creativity, innovation, and opportunities to explore the world of food," says Le. "While the work and training are long and arduous, flavorists have the satisfaction of seeing their flavors end up in products on the grocery shelves and pharmaceutical counters."

Susie Bautista is a flavorist from Olympia, Washington. She says that when people ask about her career, she has a tough time describing it. In an article on her blog, *Flavor Scientist*, Bautista writes, "I'm a flavor chemist, but it's easier to say I'm a chemist or that I work in the food industry. It's challenging explaining my work." Bautista enjoys her job very much and says that the most satisfying part is having her flavor creations used in well-known consumer products—and she has certainly accomplished that. Bautista's creations flavor dried fruit, bagels, nutritional beverages, smoothies, body-building protein shakes, and energy drinks. She has also flavored candy, soup cups, peanut butter, yogurt, ice cream, vodka, teas, coffees, doughnut fillings, pie fillings, cookies, and puddings. "My career path has been full of variety," she says.

How Do You Become a Flavorist?

Education

Flavorists must have an in-depth understanding of chemicals: how they react, what chemicals create which flavors, and how chemicals behave when combined with other ingredients. Because this is such an essential part of what flavorists do, a bachelor of science is required, preferably in chemistry, microbiology, or food science.

Once the necessary education has been completed, aspiring flavorists must complete a rigorous training process as mandated by the SFC. This usually begins with being hired by one of the flavor and fragrance companies as a laboratory technician or research assistant, working under the tutelage of a senior-level flavorist. The next step is taking a comprehensive written exam. Upon receiving a passing score, aspiring flavorists are accepted into an apprenticeship program that lasts for a total of seven years. This program is divided into two parts, the first of which lasts for five years. After completing that segment of training, flavorist apprentices take written and oral exams to test their knowledge of flavor components. Those who pass with a score of at least 80 percent move toward becoming junior flavorists and continue training for two more years. That process culminates with written and oral exams, and a score of 90 percent or higher allows the apprentice membership in the SFC.

Certification and Licensing

Once someone has completed the full seven-year apprenticeship program and has been admitted into the SFC, the person becomes a certified flavorist. This certification is not required by law but is typically a job requirement of employers who hire flavorists.

Internships and Volunteer Work

According to the SFC, many flavor and fragrance companies offer internships for college students. It can be extremely beneficial for young people who are interested in flavorist careers to perform one or more internships. They can gain valuable hands-on experience while still in college and determine whether a flavorist job is what they really want to pursue. The major flavor and fragrance company Givaudan, which is headquartered in Vernier, Switzerland, invites aspiring flavorists to seek internship opportunities, as its website states: "We're keen to support people whose passion is matched by determination. If you're bold enough to knock at our door, we may be bright enough to take you on. Try us as an intern, and experience the world of flavours and fragrances for yourself. It may just be to your taste."

Aspiring flavorists can also benefit from becoming involved with local branches of professional organizations, such as the American Chemical Society or the Institute of Food Technologies. Being part of these groups can provide networking opportunities,

Working in a culinary lab, a flavorist extracts flavor and color from carrots with the goal of matching the natural carrot flavor with a new food or drink. Flavorists are scientists who create new and improved flavors for all sorts of foods.

possibilities for job sharing, leads on employment, and internship opportunities.

Skills and Personality

It takes a certain kind of person to be a flavorist. Flavorists must be scientifically minded and highly creative. They must have an excellent memory and a keen sense of taste and smell. They need superb critical-thinking and math skills and good project management, organization, and communication skills, including the ability to listen and speak well.

Employers

Flavorists typically work for flavor and fragrance companies, which are sometimes called flavor houses. One of these is Sensient Flavors, located in Milwaukee, Wisconsin. Sensient employs twenty-five flavorists, of whom six are chief or master flavorists. Other leading flavor and fragrance companies include Givaudan and Firmenich, both headquartered in Switzerland; International Flavor and Fragrances in New York; Symrise in Germany; Takasago International Corporation in Japan; and MANE in France.

Working Conditions

Flavorists spend most of their time working in laboratories or offices. They work full time and often more than forty hours per week, especially during their early years on the job. Although the work can be stressful, most flavorists are very happy in their jobs. This is true of Charles Kaiser, a flavorist who has worked for four different flavor and fragrance companies. "I have always enjoyed the challenges of flavor creation work, and often times find myself explaining the discipline to people who never even knew the field existed," Kaiser said in a 2017 SFC newsletter published online. "They are always amazed to know what a truly fun & rewarding job it is!"

Earnings

Because of their extensive education and years of on-the-job training, flavorists are well-paid professionals. The US Bureau of Labor Statistics (BLS) does not publicize employment data specifically about flavorists, but it does have a category for food scientists. Annual salaries for these professionals ranged from $37,890 to $116,520 in 2017. On the employment website ZipRecruiter, salaries listed for flavorists ranged from $37,500 for someone at a junior level to $164,000 for senior-level flavorists.

Opportunities for Advancement

There is no doubt that the education and years of training required to become a flavorist are rigorous and require a long-term commitment. But for those who are passionate about succeeding, and who study and work hard, listen, and learn from their superiors, there are plenty of opportunities to move up from junior-level to senior-level positions. In the 2017 article on the SFC website, Bryan Quoc Le stated: "With increasing experience, skill, and talent, flavorists can be honored with even higher professional titles, such as master flavorist or chief flavorist."

What Is the Future Outlook for Flavorists?

The BLS predicts that jobs for all food scientists, including flavorists, will grow by 6 percent through 2026, which amounts to one thousand new jobs in the United States. Because most flavor and fragrance companies are located in Europe and Asia, the potential employment opportunities for flavorists could be greater than what is anticipated.

Find Out More

Flavor and Extract Manufacturers Association
1101 Seventeenth St. NW, Suite 700
Washington, DC 20036
website: www.femaflavor.org

The Flavor and Extract Manufacturers Association is the national association of the US flavor industry. Its website offers information about education and training, a flavor ingredient library, and a search engine that produces numerous articles of interest to aspiring flavorists.

International Organization of the Flavor Industry
Avenue des Arts 6
1210 Brussels
Belgium
website: www.iofi.org

The International Organization of the Flavor Industry is the global association representing the industry that creates, produces, and sells flavorings worldwide. Although its headquarters is in Belgium, its website offers a collection of news articles (in English) that might be helpful to aspiring flavorists.

Perfumer & Flavorist
Allured Business Media
336 Gundersen Dr., Suite A
Carol Stream, IL 60188
website: www.perfumerflavorist.com

Perfumer & Flavorist magazine is the leading technical and business publication for the flavor and fragrance industry. Aspiring flavorists can find a vast collection of publications on its website as well as a link to the @PandFMagazine Twitter feed, which offers more information and insight.

Society of Flavor Chemists
3301 Route 66, Bldg. C, Suite 205
Neptune, NJ 07753
website: https://flavorchemists.com

The Society of Flavor Chemists is devoted to the advancement of the field of flavor technology and related sciences. Its website offers an extensive list of frequently asked questions, which will surely be helpful to aspiring flavorists. Other website offerings include a newsletter and a number of informative articles.

Interview with a Professional Caterer

Kristin Klock-Wattie owns Root Catering, a boutique-style catering company in Rochester, New York. She has worked as a caterer for nine years, and before that she worked as an event planner in California. In January 2019 Klock-Wattie answered questions about her career by e-mail.

Q: Why did you become a caterer?
A: I was working as an event planner for a nonprofit in San Francisco. I was looking for a career change; while I enjoyed event planning, I didn't love fund-raising. I started cooking a lot at home and throwing elaborate dinner parties in my free time. That led to my desire to leave the fund-raising world and work for a catering company in the event planning/sales department. I thought it would be a good idea to go to culinary school, not necessarily because I wanted to cook, but because I wanted to immerse myself in the food scene in California. Once in school, I fell in love with cooking and did eventually go work for a catering company . . . as a cook.

Q: What was your career path to where you are now?
A: I was a psychology major at the University of Rochester and moved to California immediately upon graduation with no concrete plans (read: twenty-one years old and a burning desire to leave behind everything I knew). I started at a nonprofit as an administrative assistant and moved into the events planning department. I later moved to Boys & Girls Clubs of San Francisco as the director of special events. From there I went to culinary school and started working as a freelance catering chef, only to discover

that while I was happy, I couldn't see any real path for growth. I started working as a personal chef for a few families, which led to some small catering jobs, which led to working part time for myself under the company name "Chef k2." I moved back to Rochester in 2011 and decided that there was no one here I wanted to work for. So, in 2012 I launched Chef k2 and rebranded as Root Catering three years later when we really started to grow.

Q: Can you describe your typical workday?
A: It really does vary, which is why I love it. It's always changing too, as our company continues to grow and evolve.

From 2012 to 2016 my days were typically spent preparing for events that happened one or two times per week. That involved food shopping in the morning and cooking in the afternoon. Sprinkled in were meetings with new clients, site visits, building a new kitchen, working on our rebrand, and the launch of our new website. In 2017 we saw a big jump in business, and now my job is primarily administrative. While it still varies from day to day, I spend a large part of my day working with clients, planning events, communicating between event managers and kitchen, and now, taking on phase 2 (or 2.50), with the launch of our own event space.

Q: What do you like most about your job?
A: Days when it's moving smoothly, I love the fact that we've created this little world where I'm surrounded by people who love their job. We are passionate about what we do, we get to be creative, it feels like play, and it's a happy little space where we thrive.

Q: What do you like least about your job?
A: As with all small businesses, sometimes it's growing too fast and it's just crazy behind the scenes. There is a lot of stress in juggling this entire operation and feeling responsible for our clients, our finances, everyone's jobs, etc., etc. That being said, the worst day at Root far outweighs any other job I had on its best day.

Q: What personal qualities do you find most valuable for this type of work?

A: The ability to stay calm no matter what. Exceptional organizational skills. The drive to work hard until it's done right. Maybe just that—just work harder than you've ever worked in your life.

Q: What is the best way to prepare for this type of job?

A: If I could go back, I would have taken some basic business classes in high school or college. I would kill for Accounting 101 right now. Culinary school is not necessary to cook. Show up, work hard, don't give up, do your best, keep a sense of humor, and you'll thrive in the food industry.

Q: What other advice do you have for students who might be interested in this career?

A: Just get to work. Get into a restaurant and start cooking—but know that the kitchen is not for everyone. It attracts the oddballs, the creatives, the misfits. You'll know immediately if you are home.

Other Jobs in the Culinary Arts

Barista
Cake decorator
Cheese maker
Chocolate taster
Chocolatier
Coffeehouse owner
Cook
Cooking instructor
Dietician/nutritionist
Farmers market manager
Food and beverage manager
Food broker
Food critic
Food lawyer
Food photographer
Food public relations

Food safety specialist
Food scientist
Food truck owner/operator
Food wholesaler
Holistic health coach
Hosts and hostesses
Maître d'
Molecular gastronomist
Private club and resort
    manager
Restaurant designer
Restaurant publicist
Server
Sommelier (wine steward)
Sous-chef
Vegan chef

Editor's note: The US Department of Labor's Bureau of Labor Statistics provides information about hundreds of occupations. The agency's *Occupational Outlook Handbook* describes what these jobs entail, the work environment, education and skill requirements, pay, future outlook, and more. The *Occupational Outlook Handbook* may be accessed online at www.bls.gov/ooh.

Index

Picture Credits

About the Author

Peggy J. Parks has written dozens of educational books on a wide variety of topics for children, teens, and young adults. She holds a bachelor's degree from Aquinas College in Grand Rapids, Michigan, where she graduated magna cum laude. Parks lives in Muskegon, Michigan, a town she says inspires her writing because of its location on the shores of beautiful Lake Michigan.